Dixie's Pocket Zoo

Brave the Waves

Written by Pip Jones

Illustrated by Paul Nicholls

Dixie and Mum were enjoying themselves at the seaside.
"Fish and chips!" said Dixie. "Yum!"

"I can hear shouting," Mum said.

Dixie looked out to sea. There was a boat with people on it. The boat was sinking!

"Oh, no!" Dixie shouted.
"I will get help!" said Mum. "You stay here!"

Dixie got out her purse.
Inside were her plastic animal toys.
Dixie chose a dolphin, a seal and a pelican.

Then she said some magic words.

The animals grew and grew and grew ...
until they came to life!

Polly the pelican flapped her wings.

Sid the seal let out
a loud honk.

Della the dolphin did a dive
deep into the water.

Splash!

"Go to the boat!" Dixie called.
Sid swam under the clear water.
Della bounded over the waves.

The people got onto their backs.
Polly picked up the people's cameras,
sunglasses and bags in her beak.

Soon, everyone was on the beach.
"Phew! We are safe," said the boy.
He looked for Dixie's animals.

"Oh!" said the boy. "Where have they gone?"

Dixie's magic animals were toys again!
She picked them up off the beach and
quickly put them away in her purse.

Snap!

Mum came back. A crowd of helpers
came with her.
"How did the people get out of the sea?"
she asked.

Snap!

Dixie shrugged. Then she patted her pocket ...
and smiled.